FIRST STEPS

IN MEDITATION FOR YOUNG PEOPLE

FIRST STEPS

IN MEDITATION
FOR YOUNG PEOPLE

by

JIM WILSON

JAMES CLARKE & CO. LTD.
33 STORE STREET
LONDON, W.C.1

Published for
THE GUILD OF HEALTH
1957

Second Impression 1961

FOUNDRY PRESS LTD., BRERETON ROAD, BEDFORD

FOREWORD

THIS book is intended for use by young people.

Children from eight years old and upwards find this kind of meditation helpful but they may need the help of an older friend in starting to use the Method. If the older friend has learned to meditate it will help the child to have someone sharing in the meditation. Older children may be able to find a companion of their own age to meditate with them.

The aim is to learn to know God in personal experience on a deep level of the mind and soul.

The author wishes to acknowledge the deep debt which he owes to Miss Marion Dunlop of The Fellowship of Meditation, 3 Longdown, Guildford, who taught him all that he knows on the subject.

CONTENTS

PREFACE

Every Christian wants to be a good Christian and I am sure you do.

This book is going to help you to be one.

We all need to know God. It is not enough for us to know about Him.

This book will teach you to know Him deeply and to have His love and peace in your heart.

Then you will find how much the Christian religion helps you and how it brings happiness into your life and through you to others. So try to use one of these Meditations every day for a whole week and when you have finished go over them again several times. It may help you to keep the time of the meditation by a watch or clock.

If you find difficulties in this do write to me.

May God bless you.

JIM WILSON

C/o. The Guild of Health,
Edward Wilson House,
26 Queen Anne Street,
London, W.1.

1

DO I KNOW GOD?

God is not an old man up in the sky. He is the spirit of Life. He is greater than all that He has made. His life fills both Heaven and Earth. His Life is in all life, in the tiniest flower and in every one of the tiny cells which make up our bodies. Do you know that there are more cells in your body than there are people on earth? And God is in every one of them.

This means that God is always in us and around us. St. Paul said that, " We live and move in Him," and Jesus said, " You know Him for He dwelleth with you and shall be in you." Do you know Him?

Now be very still and quiet and say over five times —counting on your fingers, very slowly.

" *Give me knowledge, dear Lord Jesus, knowledge of Thyself.*"

At the end say: " Thank you Jesus. I believe you will teach me to know you."

2

WHAT IS GOD LIKE ?

God is like Jesus. Not to look at: but in character. That means that He is loving and kind and strong
and brave and always good. He is always working
to heal all sickness and disease and to overcome all evil.

Jesus was a wonderful friend and so is God. God's
life is in the grass and makes it grow: God's life is
in the flowers: Their beauty shows us how beautiful
God is.

God's life is to be seen in everything that is perfect
and lovely and loving and peaceful and kind and just.
Because God is at work in the world expressing Himself and showing Himself in all that is good.

So now be still and say over five times:

" Jesus teach me to know Thee now, in my heart."

At the end say: " Thank you Jesus. I know
you will teach me to know you, in my heart."

GOD IS ALWAYS IN ME

Jesus said that God's Holy Spirit would be in us. And that is true.

And because that is true you can learn to know Him within. In your own heart and mind and soul. And if you do, you will never be alone, because He will always be with you and in you and you will know it.

Then, you will have peace in your heart and never worry or get upset.

Then you will have love in your heart and you will be loving to other people even if they are not loving to you.

Then you will have joy in your heart and will be full of happiness all the day.

Then you will know that God is with you and you will never be afraid.

But if you want this to happen, you will have to learn how to meditate, and that means learning to know God deeply.

Can you now be still and quiet and say over six times:

Jesus said: " *Lo I am with you always,*" *and that means now.*

At the end say: " Yes. I believe that. Thank you Jesus."

CAN I LEARN TO KNOW GOD?

Yes; if you really want to and are prepared to give a little time every day.

It is best to get two minutes just after you are up in the morning. Or you might get it during the dinner hour break.

You will find it helps if you can learn to sit in a disciplined way. Sit in a straight-backed chair or on a stool with your back straight and head up with both feet flat on the floor and your hands on your knees. Then for a moment or two just relax and let all tightness go from your body and from your mind and from your face, so that you are not holding yourself tight at all.

Then say over ten times quite slowly in your mind: " I am now giving you My peace."

and realise that God is speaking this to you for God is Peace within you.

When you have finished say: " Thank you God."

5   LET GOD SPEAK TO YOU

Every time that you meditate, take great trouble with it. First relax. It makes a lot of difference. Get quiet before you begin to say the sentence in your mind. Then say the words slowly, letting them go deep down into your mind. Don't think what the words mean. *Don't try* to stir any feelings. *Don't try* to do anything at all, just let the words sink, because they are the truth. God is Peace and His Peace is within you and when the Word Peace goes deep into your soul it will call out God's Peace into your mind. You won't feel it at once. In fact you may not begin to feel more peaceful for some time. But it will come and then you will know the Truth.

" *I am Peace within you.*"

Say this over and over now for one minute and do this also at any time when you feel bothered about anything.

Then say :

"Thank you dear Lord that you are Peace within me."

6

WHAT WILL GOD SAY ?

God is Love and Joy and Peace and Goodness and Wisdom and Life and Health. Each of these words stand for God so they are Words of Life.

That is why these words can do great things in us if we let them fill our minds and souls. God is love within us. That is Truth: and God is Truth. So let the words sink. You must persevere with this every day. There are so many other words and thoughts which go down into our minds which do us harm: and it takes a little time before these words which speak of God's life in us go deeply enough to change the darkness in our minds into Light. When it does happen it will give you great joy and bring you to a deep knowledge of God. Say over and over again now for one minute:

" *My Peace I give unto you.*"
at the end say:

" Thank you Jesus for your peace."

WHY IS GOD'S LIFE IN ME ?

God is always within us. His Spirit and life is in all
the world and greater than the world, and yet He is in
every single person in all the world and in you now.
But why is He in everyone like this? Life always expresses itself. A live flower is beautiful. It expresses
something of God's beauty. A butterfly that is
alive expresses more of God's beauty. So God's life is
in you wanting to express itself still more in love, joy,
peace, goodness, beauty, health and in lots of other
ways. God's life is imprisoned in us if we don't let it
come out and express itself. Meditation opens the way
for God's Spirit to come out and express itself in our
lives. And it does so when we are loving, kind, happy
and full of life and health. Then we are like God and
please Him. Say over these words for one whole
minute and know that God is speaking to you:

" *My life is now within you.*"
at the end say:

" Thank you God for being Life within me."

8

IS GOD'S LIFE IN ME WHEN I AM NAUGHTY ?

Yes. He is always in you when you are good and when you are naughty. That is why our being naughty always hurts Him. No wonder it also makes us un-happy to be naughty. And His life is also in any per-son that you are rude to or unkind to. That hurts Him; not only in you but hurts Him in the other per-son as well. It is when we forget Him that we are naughty. Love goes out of our mind and so we are unloving to someone. Or we are selfish and forget Him.

Meditation teaches us to know God so deeply that we don't forget Him. And also in meditation the thought of God's love goes down into the mind and changes the badness into goodness, the darkness into light.

Now say over and over for one and a half minutes:

"*Trust only in Me and I will bring you out of dark-ness into light.*

Then say:

" Thank you God for being the light within me."

GOD IS LIGHT AND IN HIM
IS NO DARKNESS AT ALL

Light is a lovely thing: When it comes it drives away the darkness and the light shines even into the dark corners of the house. And God is Light. When His light shines in our minds and souls it drives out all the darkness—sin and ugly tempers and selfishness and unkindness and all other darkness and then we are light within. Nothing dark or ugly or cruel comes from God because " in Him is no darkness at all." God is good always. We must hold on to that Truth. God never sends sickness. He wants us to be whole. God never sends war. Nor does He ever want anyone to be cruel or unkind. All these horrid things come from sin and evil in the world.

So get very still and say over and over again for one and a half minutes:

" *Let Thy Goodness shine in me dear Lord.*"
And at the end say:

" Thank you, Father."

WHERE DOES EVIL COME FROM ?

God has made the world to be His Kingdom " on earth as it is in Heaven." He works to bring the goodness of Heaven onto the earth and He wants us to help Him to do this. But God won't force us to be good. He never has forced His creation to be good. He said: " This is the Way. Walk ye in it." And none of His creation and none of the people He has made have walked in His way. They have strayed from the right way and so have sinned. Jesus is the only man who ever lived on earth who entirely pleased God and walked in His way and did no evil. We all sin and every sin adds to the evil of the world which brings suffering to the whole world.

That is why it is only Jesus who can help us not to sin. In Him we can please God. So just say over and over again for one and a half minutes:

" *Keep me Jesus in Thyself all the time.*"
then say:

" Thank you Jesus for being so close to me."

THE JOY OF THE LORD IS
ALWAYS IN YOU

God is joy. Go out to the fields and the woods on a spring day and listen to the birds. It is God who has made them and how full of joy their songs are. Look at the primrose growing half hidden by the stream. God made it: and how it rejoices to express His beauty. So God has made you to express His joy and His beauty in your character, in love and joy and peace and goodness: and his beauty in your body, in health and in a happy face: and in your mind, in wisdom and knowledge of what is good.

Do you want to be like Him in this way? You can only do it by learning to be quiet and to let His spirit sink into your soul and mind. Then one day you will find that the love and joy and peace which you have meditated on will begin to come out into expression in your life. It can only do this if you persevere in letting it sink deeply into your soul.

So be still and say over and over again for two minutes:

"*Give me knowledge dear Lord. Knowledge of Thy Joy.*"

Then say:

" Thank you Father for everything which is lovely and good within me."

FROM INSIDE TO OUT

Most people think that the things which you can see and touch are the most important. But meditation teaches us to know that the things which you cannot see or touch are really the most important. It is what goes on in your mind which makes you laugh or makes you angry. The angry feeling inside makes your angry looks and unkind words outside. It is something funny which you think of, which makes you laugh. It comes from inside to the outside. So if you want to be happy outside you must put happy thoughts inside. If you want to be loving to people you must put love into your mind. If you want to be healthy and well you must put healthy thoughts into your mind.

This is what we do in meditation. We put into our minds thoughts of love, joy, peace, so that these may come out into our character. From inside to outside.

Can you say over and over in your mind now for two minutes:

" *God is Goodness within me.*"

Then say:

" Thank you God for being goodness within me."

13

GOD IS WITHIN AND
WANTS TO SHINE OUT

God is always all round us and in us and when Jesus came to live in this world He came out of God and showed us what God is like. In the same way the light and love of God is always round us and in us and He wants His love and goodness and peace to come out into our lives to show itself. He said " let your light shine before men." But He can only come out and shine through your life if you learn to know Him as He is within you. In meditation we try to do this : we keep very still and let the truth that He is within us sink slowly and quietly into our souls. Do not forget to relax before you begin to meditate and if you feel stiff or want to move just try to let go and relax again. It will help you to be still and quiet.

So now say very quietly for two and a half minutes :

" *Be still and know that I am Jesus within you.*"

Then say :

" Thank you, Jesus."

14

BE STILL

By now you will be learning to keep very still. You can do it without being strained. In fact the more you can relax and let go of all strain the quieter you can be in body. Then we gradually learn to be quiet in mind. When something attracts our attention we let it go—we can think about it later on. So the body and the mind become still and as the words sink into our minds and deeper into our soul we get quiet deep down inside and know that God is here and we are content to wait quietly close to Him knowing His deep love and goodness and loving Him and saying for two and a half minutes:

" *I will be still, in Thy presence dear Lord.*"

Then say:

" Thank you God for teaching me to be still and learn of Thee."

15

GOD IS LIGHT

Let the words of the meditation sink into your mind by just saying them slowly over and over again. Do not think about them, or what they mean. The words are truth. Let the truth go deep down into the mind. " God is light within me." If the light which is God's spirit goes down deeply into your mind it will begin to change anything which is dark down there. We all have some darkness in our deep minds—some hatred, or bitterness, or worry, or fear. It will help us ever so much if this darkness is changed into the light which is love and joy and forgiveness and peace. Sometimes we do not know that there is any darkness there until we suddenly have feelings or thoughts which are not good. Then we need God's light to banish the dark-ness.

So once more. Be quiet, for two and a half minutes, and listen while God speaks to you.

" *I am light within thee.*"

Then say :

" O how lovely is the light—Thank you God."

16

GOD FORGIVES

God has made us in such a way that we can grow like
Him and reflect His life in ours. We do this every time
we are loving and calm and kind and peaceful: when
we are brave and just and full of joy. You see: God
is Light: He is love and joy and peace. If ever we
are unkind, unloving, cruel or unjust or resentful or
bitter or wicked, we are not reflecting God but something which is less lovely than God or it may be evil and
darkness. Now, we live in a world which is very full
of evil and that evil affects us and we are tempted to
become evil or to sin. But God wants us to be like Him
and so, if we do what is wrong and sin, God is always
ready to forgive us, if we repent. The moment we
repent His forgiveness is ours. God loves us and He
does not keep us waiting. He forgives. So if you have
sinned say (for two and a half minutes), quietly, and
meaning it:

"*Father I am sorry. Thank you for forgiving me.*"
And then at the end:

"Now help me to be more like Thee dear Lord."

26

DELIVER US FROM EVIL

God has made the whole world and He wants it to be good, but it is not. A large part of His creation has fallen away from His purpose and is not what He wants it to be. There is a lot of evil in the world and because God is also in the world the evil hurts Him. If Jesus is always in us, anything cruel or unkind is done to Him as well as to the person whom we hurt. That is what makes wickedness so dreadful.

But God is always with us and He will keep us from evil if we trust Him and learn to know and love Him and if we think good thoughts. It will save us from hurting God and help us ever so much to be happy.

So now knowing that God's spirit is within you; for two and a half minutes try to be quiet, and rest in Him and say, but say it slowly:

" *Teach me, Jesus, to think good thoughts by Thy Spirit within me.*"

Then say:
" Thanks be to God."

LEARN TO LET GO

When you are sitting quite still, wanting to meditate, you just repeat the sentence over and over again, without thinking about the words. This is not easy at first because we want at once to think what peace is like or we think of someone we don't like when we meditate on Love. Now we must try to let go of doing this. Let go of all thought and just let the words go down into the mind. God will then be able to use the words to teach you what *He* means by peace or love. If you do the thinking, God can't speak to you. You must wait and let Him teach you. Then this will help you a lot in your life, to grow like Him.

So now repeat slowly in your mind for three minutes:

" *I will be still and let God teach me to know His peace.*"

And then say:

" Thank you God for teaching me."

I WILL LET GO AND LET GOD

We sometimes find some other people very difficult. Perhaps they order us about; or they say something which hurts us: or they are rude to us in what they say. Now what do we do? If we are rude back to them and answer them rudely or if we get angry and say unkind words, we are as bad as they are. We have allowed their rudeness or unkindness to make us rude and unkind.

What did Jesus do? He let the rude word go—He didn't answer back. When they nailed Him to the Cross He didn't curse them. He prayed for them. And so He ended the evil. It couldn't find any place in Him. Now that is what meditation helps us to do. It fills our mind with good and helps us to let go of the evil.

Try now to say over and over, for three minutes:

" *I will let go of the wrong which I want to do and let God fill my heart with love.*"

Then say:

" Thank you Jesus for what you have taught me."

DON'T LEAVE GOD OUT

So many people leave God out of their lives. Some do altogether and never think of Him and yet He is in them and round them and they don't know it.

Other people do think about God and say their prayers: but when they are in any difficulty they forget Him and start to worry and keep on worrying trying to solve their problem by themselves. They have forgotten that God is real and that He is Wisdom and can help them. If, instead of worrying, they were to be quite still and say over several times:

" *Be still and know that My wisdom is with you and will help you.*"

They would begin to know how true that is and that worry is no use at all.

In this way meditation helps us day by day. So now let go everything which bothers you and say:

" *Be still and know My power within you.*"
At the end say:

" Thank you Jesus; help me never to forget you are with me."

21

YOUR FIRST THOUGHTS ON WAKING

If you persevere you can learn to have a thought of God every morning when you wake. You will then let your heart go out to Him in Praise and happiness and this will begin every day well and help you to know how real and near God always is.

You need to have a sentence which you can easily remember. Perhaps you can use one of these:

"*I will rejoice in the Lord : for He is my God.*"

or

"*Holy, Holy, Holy, Lord God of Hosts : heaven and earth are full of Thy Glory. Glory be to Thee O Lord.*"

or

"*In My presence is the fullness of joy.*"

or

"*Thanks be to God for this New Day.*"

22

WHEN YOU ARE IN BED

It is best to kneel, before you get undressed, and to say some prayers to God. To thank Him for all that has been good during the day. To ask His forgiveness for all your sins. To commend all you love to His care: To pray for all who suffer from the evil that is in the world: To pray that His Kingdom may come on earth. Then when you are in bed say over and over as you go to sleep, hearing God saying to you:

" *I will give you rest.*"

or

" *I will give you peace.*"

or

" *My love is watching over you.*"

and just go to sleep repeating it.

WHAT DOES GOD WANT ME TO BE ?

Lastly. What are you going to be when you grow up? God only knows what He wants you to be. And as the world is His world and he has made it and as He has put you into it He must know what he wants you to do and to be. Why not meditate about it?

That is the way to open our minds to let God speak to us and tell us what He wants.

God who is so great and lovely is and always has been greater than the whole world, but He works in it to make it into His Kingdom on Earth and therefore to overcome all evil and to perfect all things.

And He wants us to help Him. So whatever work we grow up to do ought to enable us to do this: to work with Him and to help Him.

So now quietly meditate on this.

" *Teach me to know the way that I should walk in, for Thou art my God.*"

Then say:

" I thank Thee Lord that Thou wilt show me what Thou wilt have me to do."

24

IF SOMEONE YOU LOVE IS ILL

You can help someone who is ill very much by your prayers. Don't think of their illness or of their pain. First remember that God is always in you and in the person you love and He is always working to overcome the illness because He loves us all and wants us to be whole and well.

You need never beg Him to make anyone well, because He wants them to be well even more than you do.

So be still and know that God is at work. Think how entirely you can trust Him. Then say over and over in your mind:

" *I thank Thee dear Lord that Thy will is to make .... whole.*"

Later in the day—do the same and say:

" *I thank Thee Jesus that Thy love and peace are in me and in .... now.*"

Or hear God saying to you:

" *Be still and know that My life is now within, working to make .... whole.*"

IN THE END GOD WILL WIN

It is right for us to think that God is always with us and always working to heal and to overcome all evil, as we did in the last meditation, but we must also know that the power of evil is very strong and sometimes God can't do, at once, what He wants to do. Then it *looks* as if He is defeated and if we are not careful we may think He has failed. Didn't it look like that when wicked men had nailed Jesus to the Cross? His enemies mocked Him and said: " He saved others Himself He cannot save." But it was not so : He did finally triumph over all evil by Rising from the grave.

So sometimes it seems as if God had not heard our prayers. Perhaps someone we pray for dies instead of getting better. But it does not mean that God has failed. It may mean that evil has triumphed for the moment like it did for the moment on the Cross. But God is real and in the end He will triumph and we shall meet our friend again and God is with us to comfort us.

This might be a very difficult time for you but as a good soldier of Christ we must get quiet and just know that God is real and that His love will uphold and strengthen us however strong evil may be in the world.

Can you say at a time like this—over and over?

"Fear not for I am with you. I will be your strength and your comfort in every trial."

Then at the end say:

" Thank you Jesus for teaching me to know how real you are.

IF YOU ARE ILL

God is always working in all the world to put right what is wrong and therefore He is working within you now to heal you and to make you whole. If you know this, you will not be afraid. You will be very quiet and relax and just try to rest in God, knowing that His life within you is working to heal and make you whole. God never wants us to be ill. Jesus said: "I am come that they may have Life": and life is always lovely and good. God wants us to be lively members of His Body, the Church, with His life flowing through us.

So just be still and say, over and over many times:

"*I am Thy health within thee*" and again later

"*I will make you whole.*"

Do this for as long as you can and then say:

"Thank you Jesus I am getting better now with your help."

DON'T BE FRIGHTENED

There is no need for us to be frightened of anything, if we remember that God is real and that He is always round us and in us. We are never without help. Even in the darkness God is with you and He is Light and so you need not be afraid. If something makes you afraid, in the night, try to get quiet inside and say the word " Jesus " just quietly in your mind several times and then hear Him saying to you :

" *You are in My keeping, there is no need to be afraid.*"

Then if you are afraid of some person, look at the person you are afraid of and you will find he (or she) is not so terrible as you thought. Or look at the situation you are in and think—God is here and understands and I have His help now. Then set to work and do what you think is the best thing to do and you will find God will not fail you. Because, God is real and you can trust Him; say now for as long as you can easily do :

"Thou art in My keeping, you have nothing to fear."

then say :

" I do thank you Jesus."

PREPARATION FOR WORSHIP IN CHURCH

When you go into Church try to be quiet and first kneel down and say: " Dear Lord I have come to unite with all the other members of Thy Body, the Church, to worship the Father with you. Help me to take my part fully and well."

Then sit up—both feet on the floor. Hands in your lap, straight back and head up. Close your eyes. Then say slowly—over and over again—in your mind—not aloud:

" *Be still and know that I am with you and in you.*" Do this for two minutes. Then if there is more time:

" *Holy Spirit speak to me and teach me to worship Thee.*"

As the service begins, try to have an open mind so that God may teach you to know Him better.

And when the service is finished, before you leave the Church say:

"Keep me, Lord Jesus in Thyself and in fellowship with all Thy saints for ever."

THANKSGIVING FOR COMMUNION

Do you go to Communion on Sunday? If so, you go with lots of other members of the Church to make up, with them the Body through which Christ offers the bread and the wine to His Father. The congregation is what St. Paul calls "the Body of Christ" and you are part of it. In this service Christ fills the whole congregation with the communion, which is His life and strength and you as part of His Body will also be filled with His life and strength.

When you make Communion in this way, with all the other members of the congregation, you come out of Church with that Life of Christ within you. It is the food which Christ has given for His Body and you have to learn to feed on Him in your heart by faith, so that Christ may be able to work through you in the world. So be very still and quiet as soon after Communion as you can and say over and over again hearing Jesus saying to you:

"*Feed on Me, in your heart, now, with thanksgiving.*"

At the end say:

"Thank you Jesus. Keep me always in yourself that I may know that you are always with me."

IF THERE IS UNHAPPINESS AT HOME

If there is any unhappiness at home I do want you to realise how you can help. Do you know that our thoughts can either help or even hinder other people? If you are miserable or angry or even depressed, others in the house will feel it at once. And if you are cheerful and nice it helps. Other people know your thoughts. Deep down in their minds they can feel them. So if there is unhappiness in your home, try to get away where you can be alone with God and get quiet and meditate.

Hear God saying to you:

"*In My presence is the fullness of Joy*"

or just

"*Be still and know that My love is changing sorrow into joy.*"

And then when you have finished say:

" Jesus I can trust you to help me in every trouble. Thank you so much."

ARE YOU GOING IN FOR AN EXAMINATION ?

It is no good being frightened about an exam. If you have worked hard and tried to do your work well then your deep mind has got all the knowledge that you have thought of within it. You may not be able now to remember it, but it is there. If you get into a panic you will never remember it. Just resolve to do this— When you have been given your paper, look it through quickly and then get quiet for a moment, don't think whether you know the answers or not, but be still and say :

" *Dear Lord you are wisdom and knowledge now within me.*"

say it over ten times and then be quiet and say :

" *Now I have peace within me.*"

Then set to work knowing that God will help you because His spirit of wisdom is within you, helping you. And so today, at home, before the exam, say over these words now, quietly and slowly :

" *I am Wisdom and Knowledge within. Trust in Me.*"

Then at the end :

" Thanks be to God."

DISAPPOINTMENT

This world is not an easy world to live in because there is so much evil in it and it is so spoiled by sin. This is very disappointing to God because He wants it to be a happy world for us all. But God does not just become sulky about it. He looks at it and says: " I will do something about it." He looks at it and says: " I will ask—(that is you) to help Me to put right what is wrong."

And so you were baptised and signed with the Cross on your forehead to mark you as a Soldier of Christ who would " fight manfully under Christ's banner against all evil."

Are you fighting? Are you a Good Soldier? Can you take hard knocks? Can you be brave when you are disappointed and do something to make up for it and be happy?

Yes. *" I can do all things through Christ who is in me and who strengthens me."*

" I can because God can and God is in me."

Try to use that as your meditation and then say: " Thanks be to God."